Copyright © Prakash A. Raj 2001

Published 2001 by
Rupa & Co.
7/16, Ansari Road, Daryaganj
New Delhi 110 002

Offices at:
15 Bankim Chatterjee Street, Calcutta 700 073
135 South Malaka, Allahabad 211 001
PG Solanki Path, Lamington Road, Mumbai 400 007
36, Kutty Street, Nungambakkam, Chennai 600 034
Surya Shree, B-6, New 66, Shankara Park,
Basavangudi, Bangalore 560 004
3-5-612, Himayat Nagar, Hyderabad 500 029

ISBN 81-7167-571-9

Photo Courtesy:
Reuters Picture Archives and the Author

Cover & Book Design by
Arrt Creations
45 Nehru Apts Kalkaji
New Delhi 110 019
arrt@vsnl.com

Printed in India by
Gopsons Paper Ltd
A-14 Sector 60
Noida 201 301

CONTENTS

GENEALOGY OF SHAH FAMILY

KING PRITHVI BIR

KING TRIBHUWAN — Daughter (married to Keshar Shamsher Rana)

KING MAHENDRA
(married to Crown Princess Indra and Queen Ratna)
(daughters of Hari Shamsher Rana)

PRINCE HIMALAYA

PRINCE BASUNDHARA
married to Helen
(daughter of Nara Shamsher Rana)

JAYANTI   JYOTSNA   KETAKI

KING BIRENDRA
(married to Queen Aishwarya
daughter of Kendra Shamsher Rana)

KING GYANENDRA
(married to Queen Komal
daughter of Kendra Shamsher Rana)

DHIRENDRA

DIPENDRA   NIRAJAN   SRUTI

PARAS   PRERANA

PUJA   DILASMA   SITASMA

GENEALOGY OF RANA FAMILY

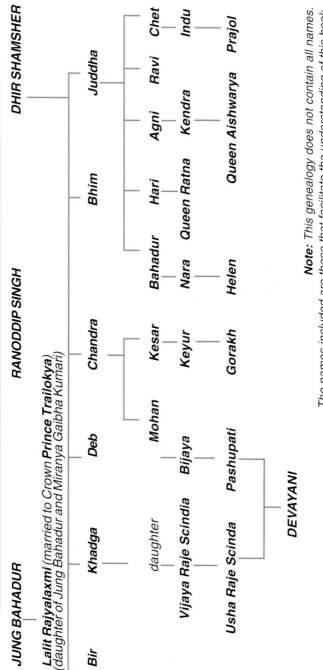

Note: This genealogy does not contain all names.
The names included are those that facilitate the understanding of this book.

PROLOGUE

"The King is dead! Long live the King!"

It is tradition that the death of a king is followed closely by the coronation of a new one. No time is lost in naming the new king because the line of succession is clear and usually based on primogeniture. The Himalayan kingdom of Nepal, in keeping with this tradition, found itself three monarchs in the space of four tempestuous days. The citizens of our nation, horrified and grief-stricken to say the least, were expected to adjust loyalties at short notice, not just once, but twice.

The chain of bizarre happenings was triggered off on that fateful night of June 1, 2001. A young Crown Prince, passionate and impetuous when crossed in love, took into his hands not just his own life, but also that of his entire family. What followed was a violent case of multiple murders, ruthless killings in cold blood, and a nation was stripped of its monarch and thrown into flux. From then till June 4, lasted a phase of "firsts" for Nepal. It was the first time the kingdom had seen three kings in four days. It was the first time a comatose man suspected of multiple murders was crowned king while his very life was flickering weakly in a hospital room. It was the first time the same man was crowned king again after a period of fifty years. It was the first time regicide, patricide, matricide, fratricide and suicide occurred on one terrible night under one, ill-fated Royal roof. The people did not know what to do. Indeed, neither did the ones who were supposedly "in charge" of the situation. Disbelief and despair caused the Nepalese public to run wild on the streets, rioting and revolting against the turn of events.

King Birendra remained King of Nepal from 1972 till his tragic death in 2001. Once it was learnt that he was dead, the Council of State *(Raj Parishad),* held a meeting the next morning at 11 a.m. The Council had to perform its function of declaring the death of one King and declare a new King. In doing so, it had to abide by the Royal Succession Act, which allows for the eldest son to succeed to the throne after the father's death. Therefore, there was really no choice for the Council. They were forced to declare that Dipendra was the new king although most people suspected him to be a murderer. For the next forty or so hours, Dipendra was the nominal King of Nepal. Nothing could be done about the fact that the twenty-nine year old man was scarcely breathing and was quite ignorant of his new status.

When he was declared dead at the hospital, there was a reaction mixed with relief, sorrow and confusion. At least now the Nepalese people did not have to accept as King a man who had committed the gruesome murders of his own family, said some. Others were sad that he died without getting a chance to tell his side of the story. Many of these people could not believe that a man could kill his own flesh and blood. They suspected a deeper conspiracy. On Monday, June 4, 2001, Gyanendra was declared the new King of Nepal. He had been declared the Regent when the unconscious Dipendra was named King. And now, Gyanendra, younger brother of the Late King Birendra, was to replace Dipendra as King. This was to be his second stint as ruler of Nepal. He had been crowned the King for a few months, fifty years ago in similar, turbulent circumstances. Not being the eldest child, it is quite unusual that he was crowned King twice in his lifetime, since the crown usually goes to the eldest male and follows that line of succession.

But Nepal was not yet ready for a new King. The people were still getting accustomed to the loss of a beloved King who had been tragically and mysteriously murdered. The Maoist movement that gained momentum at the time, taking advantage of an overwhelmed nation's vulnerability, did not help the explosive situation at all. It is small wonder that the killings of June 1 had far-reaching consequences on Nepal. The country's stability was shaken beyond belief, public opinion was divided and there seemed no solution in sight. Nepal was a nation in crisis.

THE SUN SETS ON KATHMANDU

Superstition has governed the actions of people since time immemorial. The people of Nepal are no exception to that. They have many beliefs and values that dictate their behaviour and attitudes. The night of May 31, 2001, many Nepalis slept uneasy. They complained that there were dogs wailing all night, which is interpreted as an omen of death. The foreshadowing of doom was helped by the fact that Nepal had witnessed several ill-boding occurrences in the recent past. A statue of *Bhimsen*, one of the *Pandava* brothers from the Hindu epic *Mahabharata*, had been observed to perspire over the past four months. Legend has it that the statue, located 135 kilometres east of Kathmandu in Dolakha, has been seen to sweat as an indication of a national calamity to come.

The city of Patan in Nepal plays host to an annual chariot festival in May. This marks the start of the monsoons in the region and the chariot makes a tour round the ancient city. Traditionally the King should also be among the audience as the tour draws to a close. Last year, during this auspicious journey, a part of the chariot broke, scaring the nation with the implications of such an inauspicious occurrence. This had never been a good sign. What would happen now?

However, there were no indications that the calamity would take place in the Royal household. The Queen was a pious woman, placating all the Gods and performing *pujas* whenever required. She and the King were devotees of the Sathya Sai Baba of Puttaparthy, India. The Royal couple also had the blessings of *Kumari,* Nepal's very own living goddess, a young girl worshipped by the Hindus until she reaches puberty. Her blessings had been considered crucial ever since King Prithvi Narayan Shah

▼
King Birendra and Queen Aishwarya with Sathya Sai Baba at Puttaparthy, October 1999.

Chariot of red Machhendranath which was damaged in 2000, indicating an inanspicious omen.

conquered Kathmandu on the day of *Indra Jatra* and been blessed by her. In 1954, she had placed the *tika* on the forehead of Crown Prince Mahendra instead of on the then King Tribhuwan. The King died within six months from that day. King Birendra had visited her during *Indra Jatra* in September 2000, when she had blessed him in accordance with all religious customs and rituals. Thus, the small Himalayan kingdom had little reason to anticipate a tragedy of such terrible proportions as would soon follow.

On June 1, 2001, Kathmandu was a busy city. A three-day strike against the then Prime Minister had ended only a few days ago. Life was slowly returning to normal. Vehicles jammed the streets. All shops selling essential goods had reopened. In the last decades, law and order had deteriorated in Nepal. There were reports of mugging on the roads. Tourism had suffered in this Himalayan kingdom as a result of this. Kathmandu could no longer boast of being one of the safest capital cities of the world. People were wondering if the democracy restored in 1990 had not led to pervasive corruption, lawlessness, paralysing strikes, lack of governance and deterioration of security all over the country.

The monsoons had not yet arrived in Kathmandu. Occasional pre-monsoon showers had, however, alleviated the heat and cleansed the dusty atmosphere. New Kathmandu is full of offices of airlines, travel agencies and elegant shopping areas. In the heart of this city is situated the New Royal Palace. The King had moved to this Palace with the other members of the royal family in the 1880s. The old Royal Palace was situated in the midst of Old Kathmandu, in front of Durbar Square.

It was around 9 p.m. but Kathmandu was already a quiet city. There is not much of nightlife in Nepal's capital city and there are few tourists visiting the country in June. Suddenly, people in houses near the Royal Palace heard the unmistakable rat-tat-tat of gunfire. It continued for about five minutes and the sound seemed to be originating from inside the New Royal

Palace. Such sounds were also heard at the British Embassy located northwest of the Palace. Soon several vehicles could be seen heading towards the Military Hospital at Chhauni (cantonment). As Nepal prepared to sleep that night, a tragedy had been enacted that would turn the nation topsy-turvy in the coming days.

LEGACY OF HISTORY

It is commonly said about Kathmandu that there are as many temples as there are houses and as many statues as people. It is a city full of myths and legends that make for a colourful past and present. Every little monument, each ancient building, has a fascinating tale to tell. The *Narayanhiti* Palace is said to have acquired its name through a long-ago occurrence that the people of Nepal still relate with awe.

The *Licchhavis* were the ruling dynasty in Nepal during the fifth century AD. There was, at the time, a sudden great drought that threatened to destroy the very existence of the kingdom. Desperate to find a solution to the problem, the King consulted a *Tantric* priest. The priest advised the King to offer a sacrifice of the most pious and benevolent man in the entire kingdom. The man must be singled out by his being endowed with the thirty-two *Lakshyan,* or symptoms, that are considered auspicious. Despite a nation-wide search, no man who fulfilled all these criteria was found.

Finally, the King realised that there was only one man suited to the rules laid down by the priests. So he called his son, the Crown Prince, and said, "Son, you know how our country is reeling under the effects of this drought."

"Yes, I saw you talking to the priests," replied his son.

"There is only one solution. A sacrifice has to be offered to appease the gods, and I have found the right man for this purpose. But you must perform the sacrifice. Go to the *Narayan* temple near the dry waterspout tomorrow at dawn. You will find a man sleeping there, wrapped in a blanket. You must kill that man to save our kingdom."

The Crown Prince did as he had been told. The moment he cut off the sleeping man's head with a flourish of his sword, water burst forth from the spout that had always been dry. Also, an immense thunderstorm occurred, and led to a downpour such as had not been witnessed for a long time. Thus the drought ended. And later the Crown Prince discovered that the man he had sacrificed had been his own father, the King himself. It was a double crime, albeit involuntary, of patricide and regicide. Fifteen centuries later, the instance of patricide and regicide was compounded with the evils of matricide and the extermination of a large section of the immediate Royal family of Nepal. Unfortunately, there was no rainstorm that washed away the kingdom's troubles this time.

The Narayanhiti Palace, which was the Royal Palace where the massacre took place on the night of June 1, derives its name from this sacrifice. Narayan is another name for

Vishnu, to whom the temple is dedicated. And *hiti* is the Newari word for waterspout. The temple is now located just outside the southern walls of the Royal Palace. And due to its proximity to the Palace, it is believed that the *Narayanhiti* Palace is where the incarnation of Lord Vishnu would henceforth take place. Therefore, the King of Nepal is regarded as the human manifestation and incarnation of Lord Vishnu. Years ago, people used to look forward to having *darshan* of the King as they believed that seeing him would wash away the sins they committed that day.

▼
Nepalese army soldiers patrol a street in front of the Royal Palace in Kathmandu. Police used batons and teargas to hold back an angry mob surging towards the Royal Palace.

Bust of Juddha Shamsher Rana, great grandfather of King Birendra and Queen Aishwarya at Nepal Museum.

astrologer who advised them on a suitable date for killing Ranoddip. In 1885, he was killed at the Royal Palace by four of his nephews: Bir Shamsher, Khadga, Chandra and Bhim. Khadga fired the first shot at his uncle, which is a crime close to patricide. King Prithvi Bir was then a minor and therefore unable to arbitrate against the murderers. Now the powers of *Maharaja* had been forcefully wrested by one branch of the Rana family. The sons of Jung Bahadur were exiled or killed as part of the conspiracy.

In a move to absolve himself of his sins, Bir Shamsher sent off the astrologer they had earlier consulted to Varanasi. The year was 1900 and he was ordered to perform a *yagya*, a special prayer ceremony, which would cleanse the sinner of the sins that he had committed. But as is the way with all conspirators, they continue to be traitors throughout. Khadga soon hatched a plot to get rid of Bir Shamsher. He was found out before he could do any damage and exiled first to Western Nepal and then to India. He settled in Sagar, a place in modern Madhya Pradesh in India. His granddaughter, Vijaye Raje, was married into the Scindia family of Gwalior, Madhya Pradesh. She was an important political leader in the Bharatiya Janata Party of India and her

son, Madhavrao Scindia, is now a leader in
the Congress Party. Vijaye Raje Scindia's
daughter, Usha Raje, was married into a family
in Nepal.

Bir Shamsher's brother, Chandra, turned
out to be the wisest of all the brothers. He
remained Prime Minister of Nepal for twenty-
eight years. His son, Mohan Shamsher, was
the last Rana Prime Minister, until all powers
were restored to the monarchy in 1951. Mohan
Shamsher's son, Bijay Shamsher, served as
Nepal's Ambassador to India for many years.
His death in 1953, due to an electric shock on
the Embassy premises in New Delhi, India, was

▲
Coronation of
King Birendra
(1975).
The late King
Birendra and
Queen Aishwarya
sitting on a throne
during the
coronation
ceremony.

23

tragic. He had been on good terms with Indira Gandhi, the daughter of Jawaharlal Nehru. Mohan Shamsher's grandson, Pashupati Shamsher Rana, was married to Usha Raje Scindia. Their daughter is Devayani, who is another link in the chain of tragic events.

Thus history brings us to this stage, when Nepal was a peaceful kingdom ruled by the widely revered King Birendra. The King had voluntarily relinquished his powers to the people of Nepal in 1990. There had been a massive upsurge of public opinion during the People's Movement at that time. On the 6 of April 1990, a huge crowd demanding that the king transfer his power to the people threatened to storm the palace. Wisely anticipating that this might lead to large-scale bloodshed, King Birendra silently agreed to give up his powers and thus pass on the mantle of sovereignty to the people of Nepal. In the years that followed, several people were disillusioned with their new political leaders and the corruption-ridden government of their country. The King abided by the Constitution adopted in 1990 even though the political parties did not. However, he was still considered an incarnation of Vishnu. The people's love for their monarch persevered and ran deep in their blood. The events of June 1, 2001 deprived them of a kind, benevolent monarch and a father figure.

THE LAST DAY IN
THE ROYAL FAMILY'S LIVES

Like the first family of any country, the Royal family of Nepal also had packed days. That Friday, which would prove to be the last day of several innocent lives, proved no different. It was full of various social commitments, and the Royalty must have looked forward to a relaxing family dinner. That was not to be. According to Royal custom, a family gathering was organised on the third Friday of every Nepalese month. The list of invitees was usually restricted to the King, the Queen, members of the Royal family and Royal relatives. The venue this time was Tribhuwan Sadan, inside the Narayanhiti Royal Palace Complex. It was named after King Tribhuwan, who had initiated its construction, and was now the residence of the Crown Prince Dipendra. On the 1 of

▼
King Birendra and family in early 1990s. Seated King Birendra and Queen Aishwarya (standing, L to R); Sruti, Dipendra and Nirajan.

June, 2001, the guest list consisted of twenty-seven people. Only twenty-four were able to attend the gathering eventually. The three absentees were Princess Preksha, youngest sister of the Queen, Kumar Mohan Bahadur Shahi, brother-in-law of the King and husband of Princess Shobha, and Princess Bimala Singh, one of the King's aunts. Prince Gyanendra was away from Kathmandu at Chitwan and therefore was not on the guest list at all.

At around 11:09 a.m. Crown Prince Dipendra placed a call to Supriya Shah. She was an old friend and also the Queen's preferred choice of bride for her son, Prince Dipendra. However, the Prince made it clear to Supriya that he wished to marry Devayani instead. Thus, no one was in the dark about Dipendra's intentions and he also maintained cordial relations with Supriya. She later said that during the phone conversation she had no inkling of what was to follow later that day.

In the afternoon, around two o' clock, Dipendra asked his orderly, Ramakrishna KC, to make a few special cigarettes for him. The cigarettes contained tobacco, *ganja* (hashish) and a "black substance". The orderly said that he had been making such cigarettes for almost a year now.

Dipendra had always been a sports enthusiast, and had even attended the Olympic Games in Sydney in September 2000. That afternoon he set out to inspect the Sports Complex at Sat Dobato, south east of Kathmandu. He drove the car himself and was accompanied by his ADC Gajendra Bohra and his Private Secretary Saujanya Joshi.

▼
King Birendra with brothers and sisters during festival of *Bhai Tika* in1999. Four of six brothers and sisters were massacred. (L to R); Princess Shanti, King Birendra, Princess Sharada, Prince Gyanendra, Princess Shobha, and Dhirendra.

Photo was taken early 1960s. Royal family — seated King Mahendra & Queen Ratna standing — (L to R) Prince Dhirendra, Prince Gyanendra, Crown Prince Birendra, Princess Shanti, Sharada and Shobha.

Preparations were on in full swing for an upcoming national sporting competition at the time. The Minister of State for Education and the Chairman of the Nepal Olympic Committee were there to welcome him. While looking around the swimming pool, Dipendra asked about the arrangements made to train participants for the swimming events. He wanted Nepal to win a gold medal in breaststroke swimming at the international level. However, at the tennis courts he admitted, "I know nothing about tennis!" Dipendra returned to the Royal Palace by four in the evening. He was his usual self and no

◄
Crown Prince
Dipendra

one had any reason to expect his inexplicable actions that night.

In the evening, the King and Queen were invited, along with the Crown Prince, to a tea party hosted by Nayan Raj Pandey, retired Royal Preceptor of Nepal. The occasion was his seventieth wedding anniversary. When he had been wed in 1931, his grandfather, the then Royal Preceptor of Nepal, had invited King Tribhuwan, Birendra's grandfather, to the wedding. The talk at the tea table mainly revolved around religion, as Nayan Raj Pandey later said. He had even recited a religious poem, he said. The King had only drunk two cups of tea, while Queen Aishwarya had *sel*, a Nepali dish. Dipendra had a soft drink. After spending an hour there, the Royal trio returned to the Palace around 6:15 p.m.

There are reports that Dipendra went after this to visit Devayani in the Maharajganj area of Kathmandu. Then he is said to have visited Anil Shah at his residence. He even promised to attend a dinner hosted by Sanjay and Shilpa Dugar, a family of Indian industrialists who lived near the Indian Embassy in the Lazimpat area. Dipendra's ADC and Private Secretary do not verify this account, but we do know that he did not eventually attend the dinner party.

When he reached Billiard Hall in the Royal Palace at around half past seven that evening, Dipendra saw he was the first to arrive at the venue of the family dinner. He waited for his family members to arrive. The hall was used for playing Billiards, as the name suggests, and also for hosting parties. Alone, Dipendra played Billiards for a while and also drank a few pegs of whisky. No one knows what went on in his mind in the next few hours while the terrible tragedy was enacted on the beloved Royal family of Nepal.

BLUE BLOOD SPILT

The host that evening for the Royal family dinner was none other than Dipendra himself. The Billiard Hall was located below his independent residence within the Palace Complex. It was to be an evening for the Royals alone, with no servants or bodyguards permitted to be present. The custom of having such a weekly dinner party had started after King Birendra's succession to the throne in 1972. Each week, a different venue was chosen and all the guests were invited there. Occasionally the responsibility for the dinner also came around to the King and Queen, with the venue being *Sri Sadan*, their personal Palace residence. The previous week the family had gathered at Mahendra Manzil, the home of Queen Mother Ratna. In turns, Princess Sruti and Prince Gyanendra had also played host at their respective homes. To say that Dipendra was not to be the perfect gallant host that evening would be a gross understatement.

Princess Sruti

There are, however, conflicting accounts as to how exactly Dipendra conducted himself at the dinner party, before he proceeded to gun down his entire family. There are many rumours that circle the truth and have spread by word of mouth. Since the truth is proving elusive, we may as well record the rumours and leave it to the speculation of the readers. One version believes that Dipendra waited alone in the Billiard Hall for his guests to arrive. The Billiard Hall and its adjoining areas slowly started to fill up with members of the Royal Family as the clock hand moved to show eight o' clock. The Queen Mother came over from her residence, Mahendra Manzil, which was situated within the Palace complex itself. Mahendra Manzil was named after the Queen Mother's husband, King Mahendra, who had died in 1972 and been succeeded by King Birendra. The Queen Mother went straight to a small room east of the Billiard Hall. Princess Helen Shah joined her there in a little while. She was the widow of Prince Basundhara (youngest brother of King Mahendra). Princess Helen's two daughters were expected to join the party later.

At around 8:19 pm, Dipendra demanded that his ADC bring him some cigarettes. The cigarettes he was given were of a Nepali brand called *Shikhar.* These contained *ganja* and also a "black substance", which was probably cocaine. Very soon Dipendra was finding it difficult to stand upright without support. His relatives realised that he was intoxicated. It is believed that Queen Aishwarya was incensed at his bad behaviour and blamed Devayani aloud for these negative changes in the Crown Prince. Four people carried the inebriated Prince upstairs to his room. These were his brother Prince Nirajan, his cousins Prince Paras and Kumar Gorakh, and his brother-in-law, Rajiv Shahi. All of them would survive the massacre, except for Prince Nirajan.

▲
Prince Nirajan

Other reports say that Dipendra came late for the party as he had gone to visit Devayani. He was not even there to receive King Birendra at the venue. This was an insult to Birendra since he was not only the King and the host's father, but also his guest. Birendra had walked down to the Billiard Hall from his office at Mangal Sadan, within the Palace complex itself. He usually preferred to walk this distance ever since he suffered a heart attack a few years ago and was advised plenty of exercise. When Dipendra arrived at the party in a drunken condition, his father ordered that he be taken upstairs to his room. The King then proceeded to enjoy the get-together with his relatives. He chatted with Ravi Shamsher Rana, who would later say that Dipendra was in fact not drunk that evening. Birendra also spoke to Mahesh Kumar Singh, a son-in-law of the Royal family, who explained that his wife was afflicted with gout and therefore could not attend the dinner that evening. The King reportedly sighed and said, "Gout and increased cholesterol have become hereditary diseases in our family."

In the meantime, Dipendra had been escorted up to his room, from where he called Devayani twice. The first call lasted about four minutes. Devayani later said that Dipendra talked about the inauguration of the National Sports Festival that was to be held on Sunday and asked if she would be attending the ceremony. She refused to volunteer any more information about the subject of their phone conversation. She did say that Dipendra's voice seemed to have been slurring during the call. She assumed that he must be unwell or drunk and called up his ADCs. She requested them to check on Dipendra in his room. Acting on Devayani's instructions, the ADC of the Crown Prince sent an orderly and a female attendant, *Dware Ama*, to check on Dipendra. They found him lying on the ground. He managed to get up and go into the bathroom, where they heard him vomiting. He ordered them to leave the room immediately and then proceeded to call Devayani. He wished her a good night and promised to call again the next day. This was his last telephone call.

The party was buzzing with conversation. Everyone was unwinding after a busy day and indulging in good food and drinks. The Queen Mother was in an adjoining room with Princess Helen. Most of the young members of the Royalty were listening to music. The intoxication of Dipendra was forgotten as the Royalty proceeded to enjoy the party, just as they were supposed to. Dipendra had been upstairs in his room for almost half an hour, if not more.

▲
Devayani Rana

All of a sudden, Dipendra entered the room. According to eyewitnesses he was armed and dressed in battle fatigues. He was also wearing gloves. He was armed with an MP-5, 9-millimetre sub machine gun. He fired wildly at the ceiling and the walls. The bullets ricocheted off the walls and King Birendra was hit in the neck and stomach. All eyes turned towards the King, he swayed slightly on the spot as a crimson stain spread near his shoulder. *"Kay gardeko?"* he asked, Nepali for "What have you done?" The King sank down to the ground near the Billiard table as Dipendra left the room.

Captain Rajiv Shahi, son-in-law of Dhirendra, was a medical doctor in the Nepalese army. He had been sitting nearby. He rushed to the King and, taking off his own coat,

35

tried to staunch the blood flowing from the neck. "I have also been shot in the stomach," the King gasped, his last words. Shahi assured him that it was more important to stop the bleeding from the neck and that they would take him to the hospital immediately.

Dipendra now reentered the room. He was carrying an M-16, a 5.56 calibre automatic rifle. He threw the MP-5 on the ground. In his injured condition, King Birendra tried to pick it up and shoot Dipendra with it. But he failed. Dipendra now sprayed bullets at the King.

Dhirendra Shah tried to make the raging Prince see reason. "You have done enough damage," he told his nephew. It was all in vain. Dipendra was going wild with the weapons and shooting everyone in sight. Dhirendra resorted to his knowledge of karate physically stop Dipendra. He was shot for his heroic attempt to save the other Royals. Although Dhirendra had severed ties with his Royal title and property in order to marry an Englishwoman in 1989, the ties of the heart were still strong. His attempt to stop the killer cost him his own life. He died of his wounds in hospital, three days later.

Princess Komal, wife of Gyanendra, was also shot. She fell down but scrambled away and so saved her life. Princess Shanti, Birendra's eldest sister, was hit by bullets too, and fell down. Meanwhile, Queen Aishwarya had run out, calling frantically for an ambulance and the security personnel. Dipendra was still in the Billiard Hall. He proceeded to shoot Kumar Khadga, the King's brother-in-law. His wife, Princess Sharada, was shot too, and fell beside her husband. Dipendra turned his gun next on Gorakh Shamsher Rana, Sruti's husband. Although Dipendra had aimed at his neck, fortunately he was wearing a gold locket that deflected the shot away from his neck and saved his life. Princess Sruti rushed towards him, saying, "Baba, you have also been hit!" She raised his head on her lap to comfort him. Very soon, Dipendra's bullets found their mark on her too. The Princess died soon after reaching the hospital from haemorrhage. People had trouble believing that Dipendra had shot her, as she had always been his favourite sister.

The next targets were Princess Helen's daughters, Ketaki and Jayanti. At this point of time Captain Shahi left the room quietly by jumping out of the window. Thus he succeeded in saving his own life. After having killed almost everyone in the room, the crazed Crown Prince trained his gun on Prince Paras and the three young Princesses, who were hiding in terror behind a sofa. Paras pleaded, "No, no, *Dai* (brother)!" Surprisingly, Dipendra listened to his appeal and left them unharmed. He turned towards the garden instead.

Princess Ketaki saw Queen Aishwarya in the garden, followed by Prince Nirajan, her younger son. She shouted to the Queen, "*Bhauju* (sister-in-law), don't go there." She got the impression that the Queen was determined to snatch the gun from Dipendra even at the risk of her own life. Sounds of machine gun firing came into the room as Dipendra shot down Prince Nirajan. It is likely that Nirajan was killed because he jumped into the line of fire to protect the Queen. Thus, one son died protecting his mother even as another son shot her down.

Queen Aishwarya was hit as she climbed the stairs towards Dipendra's bedroom. She may have been going up the steps to get away from him or to check if it really was Dipendra doing the killings and not an imposter who had the real Prince tied up in his room. It may have been that Dipendra was standing on the stairs and she was heading towards him to snatch away his gun and end the horror. This is all speculation, for there are no eyewitnesses to the killing of Prince Nirajan and Queen Aishwarya. The latter had been hit the worst. Her injuries had been mostly in the head. Reports said later that more than eighty percent of her brain mass was dislocated. It was a sad and gory sight.

The room where the Queen Mother had been sitting all this time was unaffected. Dipendra never entered that room, for reasons unknown. Immediately after the firing Prince Paras rushed there to reassure the frightened women. He did not want to upset Princess Helen and the Queen Mother with all the bad news at once, so he did not divulge the exact details. He did, however, say that the King had been shot. Instantly, Queen Mother Ratna stood up, insisting that she wanted to go and see for herself. She ordered that the Crown Prince be arrested and kept in his room. Dipendra's ADC now came into the room and said, "He shot himself," referring to the Crown Prince. It was revealed that Dipendra had walked away towards a bridge over a small stream. His body was discovered lying flat on the ground with a bullet wound in his head. Although unconscious, he was still breathing. No one had seen him shoot himself.

By now, security guards were rushing in and out of the room, preparing to take the dead and injured bodies to the hospital. The destination was the Military Hospital west of Kathmandu City, across the Vishnumati River. King Birendra was the first to be taken. His head was bleeding profusely all the way and when they reached the hospital at 9:15 p.m. he was declared dead. It is a painful irony that the King, an incarnation of Lord Vishnu, seems to have breathed his last while the car crossed Vishnumati River. The dead bodies of Queen Aishwarya and Prince Nirajan were transported to the Hospital. Unfortunately, Princess Sruti died within a few minutes of arriving at the hospital. The doctors were unable to help her. She was only twenty-five and had been married for five years. She left behind two daughters, one aged three and a half years and the other an infant of eight months. Princesses Shanti, Sharda and Jayanti were also declared dead when their bodies arrived at the hospital. Kumar Khadga was declared dead on arrival as well. All these members of the Royal family had died at the Palace itself and so they reached the hospital too late.

Dhirendra Shah also died at the hospital. He was fifty years old and had been married twice. His first wife was the youngest sister of Queen Aishwarya. Later he wanted to marry a British woman. He chose to give up his royal connections and marry the woman he loved. Thus he had left the Royal family in 1989 and lived in England with his wife and daughter. His three daughters from the first marriage were also at the party, but they were miraculously saved.

Thus ended that nightmarish night of June 1, 2001. There had been several tragic deaths and a few lives still flickered on in the Military Hospital, fighting a losing battle.

AT THE HOSPITAL

ADC Gajendra Bohra had been working in the Royal Palace for the past nine years. He was seated at his computer in the room reserved for the ADCs when he heard sounds of firing. He ran to the entrance and could see the Crown Prince dressed in his combat outfit. He knocked at the door, knowing it was locked. His primary duty was to protect Dipendra, but he could not see what was happening. By then others were entering the room by breaking in and Gajendra followed them in. He heard a loud, harsh sound and when he ran towards it, found Dipendra lying flat on his back in the southeast corner of a small bridge between two ponds in the garden. Another ADC called Raj Kumar Karki was not on duty that night but drove to the Palace because, as he said, Devayani had called him and asked him to check on Dipendra. Karki and Bohra seated Dipendra, Nirajan and Paras in the car and Bohra drove straightaway to the Hospital.

Only Paras would come back alive.

The Military Hospital of Kathmandu became the new focal point of the tragedy as the scene of action shifted to the Operation Theatre and the Emergency Rooms. The doctors were stunned as stretcher after stretcher was wheeled in carrying more and more members of the Royal family. The horrific drama intensified as the doctors discovered that most of those brought in had already died, and that one of the few survivors was the man responsible for this carnage.

Upendra Devakota was one of the most famous neurosurgeons of Nepal. Chief of Neurosurgery at the Bir Hospital of Kathmandu, he had been trained at renowned Neurosurgery institutes in both Glasgow and London. The night of the massacre he was at his clinic when an ADC from the Palace came to him and said, "The Crown Prince has bullet injuries and we are going to the Military Hospital." At a speed of more than eighty kilometres per hour, they made it to the hospital in four minutes. At the hospital, Dr. Devakota saw the body of a man with a Sai Baba locket around his neck. That was King Birendra, he learnt. The Queen's body was mutilated, especially her head. At that time, some doctors were trying to revive Princess Sruti. They were unsuccessful, however, because she had suffered a haemorrhage. The Crown Prince Dipendra lay in the Operation Theatre. His blood pressure and heart rate was normal. His pupils were dilated but his arms still showed signs of movement, an indication that the Crown Prince was not brain dead. The neurosurgery department is much better at the Bir Hospital in the heart of Kathmandu, but at that stage it was too risky to move the patient to a different hospital. He was placed on a mechanical ventilator as the doctors prepared for surgery. The bullet had entered his head from behind his left ear and emerged from the right side, leaving a gaping wound. Since

▼
(L to R); Crown Prince Dipendra, King Birendra, Prince Nirajan, Queen Aishwarya and Princess Sruti. An official family photograph.

Dipendra was right-handed, it became a matter of speculation why the bullet had been shot into the left side of his head *(Nepali Times, June 22, 2001).* A lot of people wondered if a few more lives could have been saved had the injured been taken to the University Teaching Hospital near the Palace rather than to the Military Hospital.

No one knew or admitted the details of the exact happenings at the time. Prince Gyanendra, brother of King Birendra, was informed at Pokhara, where he had gone after inspecting the progress on certain projects at the Royal Chitwan Park. He was Chairman of the King Mahendra Trust for Nature Conservation (KMTNC), an international, non-government organisation. A helicopter was sent to fetch him but was forced to return, as it was unable to land. Prince Gyanendra was informed about the incident and began the journey back to Kathmandu by car. At Mugling, halfway to Kathmandu, he was provided with an army escort. By the time dawn started breaking, Prince Gyanendra had completed two-thirds of his journey and was picked up by a helicopter. He reached the Military Hospital at 6 am.

Prime Minister Girija Prasad Koirala, who was then in office, had been informed the night before, two hours after the incident, that the King had suffered a "heart attack". He had been contacted by Kesar Jung Rayamajhi, the Chairman of the *Raj Parishad*, or Council of State. The King's Secretary, Pashupati Mahajan, also contacted him. The Nepalese weekly, *Samadrishti,* reported on the 17 of June that Koirala almost didn't believe the news. He called Rama Chandra Paudel, the Deputy Prime Minister, and both of them assumed that there must have been a *coup d'etat.*

Both the PM and the Secretary of the King went to the Military Hospital where they were told that some shots had been fired. Once Prince Gyanendra arrived at the Hospital the sketchy facts were revealed. The Chairman of the *RajParishad*, whose duty it is to declare the passing of one king and the crowning of another, was given the death certificates of the deceased members of the Royal Family.

There was a sense of something being horribly wrong as Nepal woke on Saturday morning. Newspapers had not printed any news about the shooting except the *Samacharpatra,* which just mentioned the shooting without going into details. Conflicting reports of the events were available to commoners who knew some employee at the Palace. The news spread, giving rise to rumours and misinformation since no one knew the truth. BBC and CNN broadcast the news about the killings on their channels that morning. People were frantically calling up their friends and relatives to see if anyone had the correct information. The Nepali radio and television channels played devotional music. People watched this in the vain hope of discovering the truth. Official news came only on Saturday afternoon. The news that the King was dead and Dipendra gravely ill confirmed their worst fears. The *Raj Parishad* declared Dipendra the new King and Gyanendra the Regent.

A CREMATION

Hindu customs require the funeral pyre to be lit by the eldest son of the deceased. It is a ceremony called *dagbatti*, involving lighting the funeral pyre for the first time. In ordinary circumstances, Dipendra would have performed the last rites of King Birendra. However, these were anything but ordinary circumstances. The dead man's son was also believed to have been his murderer. Besides, he lay in a coma at the Military Hospital. The younger son, Nirajan, who would have taken over in such a case, was also dead. Finally, Deepak Bikram Shah was chosen to do the needful. A reigning King or someone whose father is still alive cannot perform the *dagbatti*. Therefore the closest relative from the paternal side is chosen if the deceased person's son is not available.

The King, Queen and other family members were to be cremated on Saturday, June 2, 2001. The funeral was not made into a huge affair. No heads of state or government

were invited to attend it. The
funeral procession left the
Military Hospital at 5:30 pm.
King Birendra's body was
carried on a bier by Brahmins.
The Queen was carried in a
palanquin, the one in which
she had been brought to the
Palace after her wedding many
years ago. From the Hospital
located in the Cantonment
area, the procession passed
Swayambhu, the Monkey
Temple and Dallu, before it
crossed Vishnumati River to
enter the old town near the
temple of Shobha Bhagwati, a
tantrik goddess. It passed
through Thamel, a tourist area,
and Kaiser Mahal, where
Princess Sruti had lived after
her wedding. Prime Minister
Koirala accompanied the
procession until his car was
stoned by a mob chanting
slogans against him. He was

▶

People pay respect to the members of
the royal family, as the funeral
procession walk through the streets
in Kathmandu.

47

other Royal relatives were cremated further along the banks of the river. It took four hours before the ill-fated victims were fully consumed by the fire. *Ghee* was added constantly to the pyres to accelerate the process. The ashes were immersed in the river and the cremation platform was swept clean. These ashes would make their way, carried by the river, till they crossed the border into India and joined the Ganges. According to Hindu custom, all males in the family shave heads upon the death of an elder. All government officials in Nepal were asked to shave their heads as a mark of respect. This was not necessary for the non-Hindus. But many people, including some Buddhists, voluntarily shaved their heads. Even some women shaved their heads to make a statement of their grief. This was a mark of their love and mourning for the late King.

Birendra turned into a martyr for his people due to the manner of his death. He had been a liberal King who never asserted his Royal status more than necessary. Tulsi Ram Vaidya, Chairman of the Nepal History Society said, "Prithvi Narayan Shah unified Nepal on a military campaign. The campaign for national unity from the social, economic, cultural, religious and linguistic perspective was completed during King Birendra's reign."[1] He was a beloved King because he had given up his absolute powers to the people in 1990 and continued as a constitutional monarch. And in the decade that followed, Nepal saw many governments rise and fall. None lasted. In contrast to the instability of their ever-changing political government, the people of Nepal found great reassurance in having a benevolent King from a 233 year-old dynasty.

In the meantime, the first health report on Dipendra's condition was released on Sunday. It said that his condition was critical and that he was lying unconscious. The doctors anticipated that he would soon be clinically "brain dead". Prince Gyanendra, the Regent, issued a statement to the effect that, "According to a report of the incident received by us, an automatic weapon went off suddenly, injuring His Majesty the King, the Queen, Prince Dipendra, Princess Sruti, Prince Nirajan, and

▼
Smoke rises into the night sky during the cremation of Nepal's royal family members in Kathmandu, June 2, 2001.

other Royal family members and relatives." Dr. Devakota asked the Regent, Gyanendra, whether they should allow Dipendra to continue indefinitely on a ventilator or to let nature take its own course. The Regent discussed the matter with the Queen Mother and told the doctor to keep on treating Dipendra. But all medical attention was in vain. The Crown Prince died at 3:45 a.m. on Monday, June 4. No coins or stamps were issued depicting him as the King of Nepal, a common custom in the country. Contrary to tradition, he was taken to the cremation ground in a vehicle, while Kathmandu was forcibly silent under an imposed curfew. Gyanendra was soon declared the new *Nepal Naresh* or *Maharajadhiraj,* the King of Nepal.

Queen Mother Ratna went to visit the survivors at the Military Hospital. She looked in on Princess Shobha, Kumar Gorakh, Dhirendra Shah and Princess Ketaki Chester. It was later reported that when shown the room where Dipendra lay, she did not enter it.[2] While recovering from her injuries at the Military Hospital, Princess Shobha Shahi kept asking if Dipendra was still surviving. When she was informed that he had died, she insisted that all photographs of him be removed from her home. She did not want to be reminded of his existence when she arrived home from the hospital.[3] After that night of horror, it is understandable that few of the survivors want to remember Dipendra. Although they must be thankful to have emerged from the ordeal alive, they can never overlook the near and dear ones they all lost. Tragically, whatever they may do to erase the memory of Dipendra from their bruised hearts, they will never be able to forget his final deed.

A CROWNING

The Historic Old Royal Palace of Kathmandu, located at Hanuman Dhoka, near Durbar Square, witnessed a coronation ceremony after almost thirty years. This was the old Palace of the Malla kings, and the Royal family had lived here since the time of the first Shah King, Prithvi Narayan Shah, in 1768, till the 1880s, when King Prithvi Bir shifted into the new palace. *Nasal Chowk,* the courtyard of this monument to the Shah dynasty, is the venue for all coronations. In the audience were all high-ranking officials, including the Prime Minister, the Chief Justice, the Speakers of both houses and the Leader of the Opposition. Gyanendra inspected the Guard of Honour given by the Nepalese Army. He was clothed in the traditional Nepali dress, the *daura suruwaal,* a dark grey dress and black cap. The *Badaguruju* (the Royal Preceptor of Nepal), Kesari Raj Pandey, crowned him. All officials present offered the new King their best

A view of Nasal Chowk in old Royal Palace just before crowning of King Gyanendra.

Crowning of King Gyanendra.

King Gyanendra after enthronement. Bada Guruju Kesari Raj Pandey paying respects.

wishes and presented him with the customary coin.

After the ceremony, the new King was taken to the new Royal Palace in a resplendent six-horse carriage. Seated next to him was Prajwal Shamsher Rana, the Commander-in-Chief of the Royal Nepalese Army and the great-grandson of the Rana, Prime Minister Juddha Shamsher. The Prime Minister at the time, Girija Prasad Koirala could not be seated in the carriage with him as his life had been threatened since the events of June 1. The Royal carriage passed through the narrow alleys of Old Kathmandu before it emerged onto the broad avenues of the newer sections of the capital city. The New Road, part of the Royal route, was so called because it had been constructed afresh after the earthquake of 1934. Despite precautions, boys with their heads freshly shaved shouted slogans against the new King and the Prime Minister. People were not yet ready to accept a new King while they were still mourning an old, much-loved King Birendra who had been snatched away from them too soon.

His Majesty King Gyanendra Bir Bikram Shah Dev's accession to the throne.

King Gyanendra riding on a carriage after the crowning ceremony at the old Royal Palace.

The mourning period continued for thirteen days, as per the Hindu custom. Eleven days after the King's death, a *katto* ceremony is traditionally performed in Nepal. Ordinarily, no Brahmin will consent to perform this ceremony and to be then called a *katto* Brahmin after that. This is because the Brahmin to perform the *katto* loses his caste as a result. Thus, only a very poor, needy Brahmin ever

consents to undertake this task. During the mourning period, the Brahmin chosen for this purpose is fed delicious food of eighty-four varieties, known as *chaurasi byanjan.* This is described even in the scriptures. It is even rumoured that this food has the bone dust of the cremated King mixed into it. This Brahmin receives many gifts, including a bed, furniture, utensils, ornaments and even a Royal costume made of brocade. He is also provided with a pair of shoes and an umbrella in case it rains during the departed soul's journey to the next world. Then the Brahmin is made to wear a replica of the Royal Crown and placed on elephant back. After that he is chased across the Bagmati River, which is the boundary between Kathmandu and Patan. Thus, he is exiled forever out of the Kathmandu Valley. This elephant that he rides is gifted to the Brahmin. In earlier times, the Brahmin used to auction off this special elephant after the ceremony to landowners in the Terai region. However, this time the Brahmin was instructed to sell the elephant back to the government at the nominal price of ten thousand rupees. The Brahmin who ate *katto* for Dipendra was dressed in brocade with a replica of the Royal crown on his head and seated on elephant back. Then he was chased across the river. Strangely, the elephant kept refusing to cross the river. The *mahout* kept goading the animal before it finally crossed over. It is ironic that the *katto* Brahmin got to wear a replica of the Crown that was never to grace Dipendra's head. The elephants that were to be used for completing the *katto* ceremony for the two dead Kings had been brought walking all the way from the Royal Chitwan National Park. On the way, the elephant designated for Dipendra's *katto* had

◄
Durga Prashad Sapkota, a Brahmin priest is helped by a royal palace official during the "katto" ceremony in Kathmandu June 11, 2001. Sapkota, a Brahmin priest, the holiest figure in the Hindu faith, broke one of the ancient religion's most sacred taboos in order to assume the woes of a troubled royal palace. Dressed to appear as a likeness of slain King Birendra, the priest - a vegetarian all his life - ate a meal laced with animal marrow before leaving on elephant back on self-imposed exile in a remote part of the Himalayan mountain kingdom.

◄
Furniture being gifted to Brahmin on the eleventh day after King Birendra's death.

▶
A Brahmin priest, Devi Prashad Acharya, (C), crosses the Bagmati River on an elephant on the outskirts of Kathmandu June 14, 2001 after performing the *katto* rite — reserved for monarchs who have met tragic ends. The elephant chosen to convey Nepal's Crown Prince Dipendra's spirit into exile at first refused to cross the Bagmati river then trumpeted wildly before turning tail and chasing a group of dignitaries up a narrow path. They scattered in panic, leaving a trail of slippers and Nepali caps.

crushed a poor woman to death. She had merely gone up to the animal, which Nepalese regard as incarnations of the Hindu god *Ganesh*, to ask that she be blessed with a child. Thus even the rituals marking the death of Dipendra were fraught with misfortune and tension.

QUESTIONS: RAISED AND UNANSWERED

King Gyanendra was crowned on 4 June, 2001. One of his first decisions was to set up a committee that would inquire into and investigate the murders of the members of the Royal family. The members of this committee were Chief Justice Keshav Prasad Upadhayay, Speaker of the House of representatives Tara Nath Rana Bhat, and the Opposition Leader, Madhav Nepal. The Opposition Leader was from the Communist Party of Nepal, United Marxist-Leninist. Madhav Nepal withdrew from the committee the next day on the grounds that he was facing opposition from his own party. The two-member committee continued with its investigation. They eventually submitted a report to King Gyanendra who passed it on to Prime Minister Koirala. The PM made the report public as soon as possible. That day, there was hardly a person in all Nepal who did not listen to

▼
Nepal's new king Gyanendra (R) walks together with Nepal's Prime Minister Girija Prasad Koirala at the Hanuman Palace in Kathmandu. Nepal proclaimed its second new king in two days naming regent Prince Gyanendra as monarch.

that report on the television or radio with rapt attention. Those who did not have a television or radio of their own sat in their neighbours' houses throughout. The Speaker, Tara Nath Rana Bhat, had briefed the press.

The investigation team had visited the site of the massacre and interviewed witnesses including members of the Royal family, the ADCs of the family, doctors and other military or non-military visitors to the Royal Palace. For the first time in the history of Nepal, an investigation team stepped into the Royal

Palace and interrogated members of the Royalty. However, the report they presented did not satisfy many people. There were many questions left, but no one to answer them. The leading national daily of Nepal, the *Kathmandu Post*, summarised the report. It said that undoubtedly Dipendra had killed his family members, turning on all of them in turn with his guns. But many people refused to believe this. They could not accept that their Crown Prince had killed his own flesh and blood. The biggest question doing the rounds was, "But why?"

Other than the fact that it was hard to

▲ Nepalese demonstrators throw stones at riot police during an anti-monarch demonstration in Kathmandu on June 4, 2001. Although newly crowned King Gyanendra earlier promised a full investigation, hundreds of Nepalese tried to storm the palace, clamouring to know how King Birendra, Queen Aishwarya and six of their closest relatives came to be killed.

believe that Dipendra had committed such a heinous crime, there were also certain problems that came up in attributing the blame to the Crown Prince. For one, he had been unable to stand without help at around half past eight and had been carried up by four persons. How could the same man be able to cold-bloodedly kill so many in the next hour? Also, he never spoke at the time of the killing. He never shouted or quarrelled with anyone. Kumar Gorakh, in his testimony referred to a man who "looked like Dipendra", as he was not sure if the man was indeed Dipendra. Queen Aishwarya may have believed that the man killing the Royal family was not Dipendra and had been shot while running up the stairs to Dipendra's room. She was probably going to check whether Dipendra was lying in his room while an imposter murdered all those people. Most importantly, there are no eyewitnesses who can testify that it was Dipendra who killed his mother and his brother, Prince Nirajan, and finally himself.

A Nepalese woman carries the family portrait of the late Nepalese royal family on the 13th day of the purification ritual in Kathmandu, June 16, 2001.

Some facts also raised eyebrows when they were reported. No one can explain why the injured and the dead were taken all the way to the Military Hospital when the Teaching Hospital of Tribhuwan University is only three minutes away from the Palace. Also, the doctors at the Hospital did not perform autopsies on any of the bodies. None of the weapons had any fingerprints on them, because the murderer had been wearing gloves at the time. While that does not rule out Dipendra as the guilty party, it cannot be taken as evidence that he was the killer.

An interesting theory has been propounded by Richard Morley, a foreign observer, and was published in the *Kathmandu Samacharpatra* on the twenty-fourth of June. He suggests that Dipendra's blood should have been analysed for the presence of any alien substances. He believes that the "black substance" in the cigarettes that were specially prepared for the Crown Prince could be an intoxicant. It is certainly not opium because the effects of opium as commonly observed

▲

A Nepalese man salutes in front of a picture of King Birendra and Queen Aishwarya displayed on the street in Kathmandu.

▼
Captain Rajiv Rai Shahi, the son-in-law of the late King's brother Dhirendra describes what happened during the palace bloodbath during a news conference at the military hospital in Kathmandu, June 7, 2001. Rajiv said on Thursday the late crown prince Dipendra staggered and fell occasionally as he drunkenly mowed down most of his family in just over a minute.

were not noticed in Dipendra that night. Opium brings peace and placidity, whereas Dipendra's actions were the exact opposite of that. Morley said that it might have been Fancilidin (PCCP or angel dust) that was added to the cigarette. It was traditionally used to make one feel more courageous and helped soldiers make the first attack in times of war. Even 8 mg of Fanicilidin in a cigarette could cause vomiting, dizziness and make the addict destructive, homicidal and suicidal. These symptoms were those displayed by Dipendra according to most reports, so the idea cannot be disregarded.

There are quite a few takers for the conspiracy theory. They believe that while Dipendra was lying in his room after being carried there by his relatives, a masked man similar in physical appearance to the Crown Prince entered and shot him dead. Later he arranged the body near the lake to make it look like suicide. He proceeded then to kill the Royal family members.

Nepalese speaker of parliament (R) and an aide display the guns at a news conference in Kathmandu used by the then Crown Prince Dipendra to assassinate the royal family.

But there is a very important reason why Dipendra cannot be completely dismissed as the prime suspect. It later came to light that he had been having disagreements with his parents over his choice of bride. He wanted to marry Devayani against the wishes of his parents. Angry words had been exchanged on several occasions and the Queen had even

Nepali citizens living in Bombay mourn the death of the royal family.

66

threatened that she would ensure that Dipendra did not get to sit on the throne of Nepal. Matters had not yet been resolved the night the ruthless massacre took place in the *Narayanhiti* Palace.

There is an unofficial story being told in Nepal that several people seem to believe. It is said to be the story eyewitnesses told off the record. The weekly newspaper, *Ghatana ra Bichar,* published an article based on this version in its issue dated July 11, 2001. The story suggests that Dipendra pretended to be drunk that night so that he would be taken up to his room. He had apparently planned for some time to kill the King, his father. He later came downstairs in his battle fatigues as it was easier to carry weapons in such dress. After shooting King Birendra once he apparently shouted, "I have now become King!" Now he left the Billiard Hall to call Devayani. But just then he heard the King tell Rajiv Shahi that he had also been shot in the stomach. Upon realising that Birendra was not yet dead, the Crown Prince rushed back into the Hall to shoot him dead. He threw his first weapon down in the hope that someone else might pick it up and leave his or her fingerprints on it, thus making it easy for Dipendra to accuse someone else. He himself was wearing gloves. Dipendra allegedly shot everyone who was sympathetic toward King Birendra as well as anyone who tried to stop him, such as Dhirendra. He is believed to have laughed loudly after killing his mother and brother Nirajan. Since Dipendra was right-handed and the bullet wound on his body entered from the right, it is possible that one of the ADCs shot Dipendra. His good friend, ADC

Raju Karki was leaving for the USA in two days time. The Crown Prince was supposed to have become very lonely ever since the family opposed his marriage plans. He did not want to give up his rights as a Crown Prince in order to marry the woman he loved. His uncle, Dhirendra had sacrificed his claims to Royalty in order to marry an English woman. But Dipendra had seen Dhirendra face financial problems and was probably wary of repeating his uncle's mistake. According to this theory, no one could stop Dipendra as he had proclaimed himself King. And as per tradition, that is the rule. The real happenings of that night are a mystery that may never be solved.

DEVAYANI:
LINK IN THE PUZZLE

Devayani, the grand-daughter of Vijaye Raje Scindia and the woman for whom Dipendra seems to have destroyed his family and himself, is another link in the puzzle that the people of Nepal are still trying to piece together and will probably never solve. She has remained elusive throughout the investigation and avoided the limelight. It is still rather unclear exactly why the Royal family were against a marriage alliance between Dipendra and Devayani. After all, she is also from an illustrious family, well-connected in both Nepal and India.

Devayani's genealogy has already been explained earlier. When Chandra Shamsher had been Prime Minister and *Maharaja* of Nepal, he had been very keen on a marriage alliance between the Ranas and the Shahs. However, at that time he had no daughters eligible to marry the then King

Tribhuwan. If Devayani and Dipendra had been able to marry each other, a descendant of the Chandra Shamsher branch of the Rana family and the Shahs would one day ascend the throne.

▼
Devayani Rana, (L), sits with her sister and Vijaye Raje Scindia (C).

Chandra Shamsher Rana had eight sons. Kaiser, Singha and Krishna were three of these boys for whom he had arranged marriages with the Royal Princesses, the daughters of Prince Prithvi Bir. Of these brothers, Kaiser Shamsher Rana was a scholar and had large private libraries. All his books are preserved in the Kaiser Mahal across the street from the Royal Palace. He had another wife besides the royal princess. His grandson in the lineage from his second marriage was Kumar Gorakh, husband of Princess Sruti. Gorakh was the second cousin of Pashupati Shamsher Rana, Devayani's father. Thus Devayani was already related to the Royal family through marriage.

Devayani is a Hindu name found in the ancient scriptures. She was the daughter of Shukracharya, the Brahmin guru of the *asuras* (demons), who were constantly at war with the *devatas* (Gods). Shukracharya knew the magic art of bringing the dead back to life, the *Sanjivani Vidya*. Since he used this knowledge to revive all the demons, the gods realised they were fighting a losing battle. They sent one of their own party, Kach, to learn the *Sanjivani Vidya* from Shukracharya. The Brahmin, however, refused to impart this wisdom to the rivals of the *asuras*. The demons killed Kach. Devayani pleaded

▲
"Bijay Bas" —
Devayani's home
in Kathmandu.

with her father to revive him and teach him the *Sanjivani Vidya* so that his mission was fruitful. She had fallen in love with the *devata*. On being revived Kach thanked his newfound guru profusely and prepared to leave. Devayani implored him to stay on and marry her. But he declined, insisting that the daughter of one's guru is like a sister and one must not have any other relationship with her. Devayani cursed

71

him so that he could never put his new knowledge to any use. Kach in his anger cursed her that she would be forced to marry someone from a lower caste, which was unthinkable. Eventually, Devayani had to marry one King Yayati, who, though of noble blood, was not a Brahmin.

It seems that the curse carried on to this namesake of the ancient Devayani. Her relationship with Dipendra was under fire throughout and no happy end came of it. The Royal family objected strenuously to his decision to marry her, led by Queen Aishwarya herself. There are several views on why the relationship met with disapproval. Various newspapers have speculated over the matter in the recent past.

According to some reports, Queen Aishwarya's objection was that Devayani would dominate Dipendra instead of being dominated like all the daughters-in-law of the Royal family so far.[4] Devayani was educated, sophisticated and independent-minded, and would not appreciate or entertain interference in her life by the elders of the family. Devayani also had no brothers. The Queen's fear was that she too, would produce no male heirs to the throne of Nepal. It is also believed that astrologers had advised the Queen not to allow Dipendra to marry till he was at least thirty-five, since marriage before that would lead to a great disaster in the Royal family.

Devayani had, however, been considered eligible for marriage to Dipendra at one point of time. Queen Aishwarya's mother, Rajya Laxmi Rana, had the duty of finding a bride for the Crown Prince. She had narrowed her choices down to Devayani, Garima Rana (cousin of Gorakh) and Supriya Shah. When they asked Devayani's mother about the match in a discreet manner, she replied that Devayani was the "grand-daughter of Vijaye Raje of Gwalior, well-known for her wealth." She seemed to think that the Nepalese Royal family was poor in comparison to Devayani's family. In the eyes of the Royal family of Nepal, that ended the matter of Devayani marrying Dipendra.

Even so, some newspapers reported that Dipendra had already married Devayani in a temple *tika* ceremony instead of the usual rituals. *The Hindustan Times* of India also reported that the Queen had suggested to Dipendra that he marry the bride she chose for him and keep Devayani as his mistress.[5] Such an idea would have been rejected outright by Devayani, had it ever been put forth by Dipendra.

A Nepali weekly also suggested that Devayani's family in India had arranged for a *tantrik* to visit her in Kathmandu.[6] He is believed to have given her a gold ring studded with diamonds, which she presented to Dipendra. It implies that perhaps the love between Dipendra and Devayani was induced through a powerful spell cast by the *tantrik* on the diamond ring.

Whatever be the reason, the Royal family did not want Dipendra to marry Devayani at any cost. At first only the Queen was against the idea, but soon King Birendra also sided with her in this matter. They tried to reason with Dipendra not to do so. Some years ago, his Uncle Dhirendra had relinquished his rights and properties as a member of the Royal family in order to marry a British girl he was in

love with. He left Nepal and settled in England. The King and Queen suggested that Dipendra do the same if he insisted on marrying Devayani. If Dipendra refused to do that too, they would be forced to pass on the Crown to Dipendra's brother, Prince Nirajan.

As we already know, these threats did not change Dipendra's mind. In fact, the last ever phone call he is known to have made was to Devayani. She had also called Dipendra in the last thirty minutes of his life from her cellular phone, as was learnt upon tracing phone calls to and from the Palace. The Investigation Committee wanted to hear Devayani's account before they submitted a report. She had, however, already flown out to Delhi the day after the massacre,

presumably to avoid media attention. She was not left alone, as she desired. Instead, she was persuaded to give her testimony at the Royal Nepalese Embassy in New Delhi, in the presence of Dr. Bhekh Bahadur Thapa, the Nepalese Ambassador to India, and Dr. S.K. Jain, her physician. The following is an extract from the interview that was published in the Report formed by the Committee:

◄
Fire and Ice, and

▲
Bhat-Bhateni super market in Kathmandu — meeting place betwen Dipendra and Devayani.

> Ambassador: *Why are you in Delhi?*
>
> Devayani: *(sobbing) I am here for my treatment…I have not been feeling well.*
>
> Ambassador: *Do you have any knowledge about what happened on Friday night at the Royal Palace in Kathmandu?*

Devayani: *(sobbing) I don't have any knowledge about other things. I don't know. I had no idea it could be like this.*

Ambassador: *What do you have to say about the saying that there was a relationship between yourself and the Crown Prince?*

Devayani: *(sobbing) It's personal, I don't want to talk about it.*

Ambassador: *It was found from the Royal Palace telephone log that you had a long conversation with the Royal Palace. Can you recall and tell us whom you spoke to and what you talked about?*

Devayani: *As I can recall, the Crown Prince called me after 8 pm. He asked if I would be coming to the inauguration of the National Sports Festival on Sunday. He had called on my mobile phone and I could not hear very well. So I told him, 'I don't understand.' Then he hung up before I could answer. So I called him. He didn't lift up the phone. When he was not answering the phone it would be automatically transferred to the ADC on duty. So it was transferred. I told him that the Crown Prince's voice was slurry and to check in his room as he might not be feeling well. Then I hung up. Later the Crown Prince called again. He said he'd call tomorrow. Then he said good night. Then he asked again. He hung up before I could reply. Then I called again. Then he said, 'I am about to sleep. I'll call you again tomorrow morning.' Then he hung up.*

Ambassador: *When you were talking to the Crown Prince did you find any difference in him or was he as usual?*

Devayani: *His voice was slurred and as I said earlier he might not have been feeling well. That's why I requested the ADC to go to his room when I called.*

Devayani's testimony is confused and not very clear. The duration of the call as recorded by the Telecommunications Department was four minutes. But the conversation Devayani remembers could not have taken that long. They must have spoken about something else as well. It is quite impossible for us to ever know what that something may have been and whether it could have thrown some light on Dipendra's subsequent actions.

At the time of the massacre Devayani was attending a dinner party hosted by Sanjay and Shilpa Dugar, an Indian couple in Kathmandu. This is the same dinner that Dipendra too had promised to attend but ultimately skipped. Devayani reportedly told someone, "He is in a foul mood." Since the venue of the dinner was not far from the Palace, gunshots were heard even by the guests here.

It is not clear why Dipendra was "in a foul mood". It is commonly supposed that the question of his marriage was discussed at the gathering of the Royal family and created an angry atmosphere. But the testimony of only one witness suggests that. Prince Paras said that Dipendra talked about his desire to marry Devayani with Queen Aishwarya and Queen Mother Ratna. Both of them refused to allow the alliance. Apparently, Dipendra was supposed to discuss the matter on Sunday, two days later, with the King. The Crown Prince was to turn thirty in another three weeks. For the first time in the Shah dynasty the heir to the throne was still a bachelor at that age.

PRESUMED GUILTY

It seems to be very difficult to discern the truth in this entire tragic affair. People are speculating till date about the guilt or innocence, as the case may be, of Crown Prince Dipendra. Few outsiders know what kind of a person he was or what he was like to talk to. In the aftermath of the massacre, we are getting to hear conflicting accounts of Dipendra the man. Different people have different things to say about him.

Birendra and Aishwarya had been married in a colourful ceremony in February 1970. Dipendra was the first child of the then Crown Prince Birendra and his wife Aishwarya. He was born on June 27, 1971. He was named Dipendra, which is a Sanskrit name. The word

Queen Aishwarya during her wedding in 1970.

deep symbolises candlelight. And the suffix *indra* means *Lord of Candlelight.*

At the time of his birth, his grandfather, King Mahendra, was the absolute monarch of Nepal. At that time, political parties were outlawed in Nepal and the *panchayat* system functioned under the leadership of the King. King Mahendra passed away on January 31, 1972. It is usually considered a bad omen for a newborn in the Royal family if a family member passes away in a short space after the infant's birth. His eldest son, Birendra, succeeded Mahendra. He declared Aishwarya Rajya Laxmi Devi Shah as the new Queen and the tiny Dipendra as the new Crown Prince.

Dipendra studied in Kindergarten at the *Kanti Ishwari Shishu Bidyalaya.* This was a public school named after his two great-grandmothers, who were still living at the time. The school stands on the banks of the River Bagmati, near a statue of King Tribhuwan, Dipendra's great-grandfather. Tribhuwan was the King who had overthrown the Rana regime in Nepal and brought about democracy in 1951.

▲
Wedding photograph of Crown Prince Birendra and Crown Princess Aishwarya, February 1970.

79

▲

The *Budhanilkantha* School where Dipendra studied.

Although Birendra had completed his schooling at a Christian missionary school in Darjeeling, India, Dipendra studied in Kathmandu itself. The *Budhanilkantha* School was modelled after British public boarding schools. Dipendra studied here from class four onwards. He was treated at par with the other students. He stayed in the hostel like everybody else and led a normal life. It was only when the students got one day off each month that he was driven off to the Royal Palace while the other children went to their homes.

To make sure that the school remained egalitarian, the students were known by their first names and a number. Their last names were not used as these would give away one's caste status and bring about an unspoken social hierarchy. Dipendra was number 832. The school was still partly under construction and so, students often helped with brick-laying work and other tasks. Dipendra was also one of these students. He was involved in football and theatre. He even participated in a production of *Macbeth* while at school. His classmates say that he was also an expert in folk dancing. He used to ask the guest speakers many questions, without fail. He stayed in Nilgiri House, named after one of the famous Himalayan peaks in northern Nepal. His roommate, Harihar Joshi, remembers him as a gentle mind fond of adventure films. Dipendra apparently enjoyed reciting poems and essays. He had a good memory although he was not a brilliant student. He had started a group called *Seven Stars,* including boys of his own age.

▼
Former Crown Prince Dipendra is seen boxing with a fellow school mate at Budhanilkantha school in Kathmandu.

One of these boys remembers an incident when they saw an old man walking past the low walls of their school who fell into a ditch. Dipendra jumped across the wall and helped him to get up. He even gave the man six rupees to buy necessary medicine. The money was all Dipendra had saved from two weeks of his pocket money. Dipendra used to make it a point to stop his car and wish his teachers even when outside the school grounds. The catering assistant said that he never used to complain about the food. [7] His school friends say Dipendra was always keen on being treated like any other student. He did not object to being punished for his mischief and often had to work in the school garden before classes as part of that punishment. The guards, peons and other employees of the school used to call him *Timi*, instead of by his real title. He used to look after his younger brother Nirajan and sister Sruti very responsibly when they came to study at the same school. He liked to write poems and recite them, and to have his teachers read them. Even when he visited the school for a reunion he objected to being referred to by the honorific title of *Sarkar.*

Crown Prince Dipendra.

A temple of the *Sleeping Vishnu* was located near the school. Dipendra wanted to visit that temple. It is supposed to be forbidden for a King to visit any Vishnu temple, as he himself is an incarnation of Vishnu. The only exception to this rule is the replica of the

Sleeping Vishnu located at Balaju, a place to the northwest of Kathmandu. His classmates had to forcibly prevent Dipendra from going to that temple.

▲
"Sleeping Vishnu" at Budhanilkantha.

Khurendra Shahi was a friend of Dipendra's at this school. He was from a town in the eastern foothills of the kingdom, Dharan. He used to stay in the same hostel as Dipendra.

Nepal's King Birendra and Queen Aishwarya decorate Crown Prince Dipendra during his coming of age ceremony at the Narayanhity Royal Palace in 1990.

He recounts how Dipendra recognised him even in a crowd after fourteen years. Dipendra had gone to visit Dharan during its centenary celebrations in the year 2000. Khurendra had told the organisers of his town that he had been in school with the Crown Prince but they did not give him a chance to meet him during the ceremony. So Khurendra waited near the building where Dipendra was staying. Dipendra saw his school friend and stopped the car. He got out and said, "Where have you been, Khurendra? I have been trying to find you since I came to Dharan for earthquake relief work in 1988." Dipendra even asked him to come and say good-bye at the helipad the next day. Khurendra also visited Dipendra at the Royal Palace five months ago and talked with him for a long time. He says Dipendra confessed to being worried about his father's health and heart condition and that the Crown Prince loved his brother and sister very much.

Dipendra's exposure to a simple life at the *Budhanilkantha* School was a blessing. Instead of growing up in the isolation and importance of the Royal Palace, he interacted with children his own age from various backgrounds. His class consisted of children representing all communities and ethnic groups of Nepal. There were Newars, Brahmins, Rais, Sherpas and Dalits to name a few. For the first time, perhaps, in the history of the Royal family, the Crown Prince had the chance to interact with people intended to be his subjects in future years. Everyone he knew at school has something positive to say about him. A condolence message appeared in the Nepali daily *Kantipur,* thirteen days after Dipendra's violent death. The message contains all his school friends' names as well as the numbers by which they were known in those years. It says, "King Dipendra, No. 832, we are all shocked by your untimely and unnatural death. We memorize those unforgettable days spent in *Budhanilkantha* School and pray for the peace of your departed soul."

Eton was the next step in the Crown Prince's education, where his father had also studied. The general impression of Dipendra that one forms from speaking to his acquaintances here is not so unequivocally positive. Edward "Bear" Grylls,

▲
Smoke rises up during the cremation of Nepal's King Dipendra in Kathmandu. Dipendra's body was carried in an open army truck through streets emptied by a curfew imposed earlier in the day.

a classmate who had conquered Everest at the age of twenty-three, shared a course in karate with Dipendra. He remembers him as a "kind, gentle person". According to him, Dipendra had a small group of close friends and loved outdoor sports. He met Dipendra in Kathmandu some years later and the two had gone out for pizza. Another classmate said that Dipendra had in him a streak of "physical aggression". A classmate who teased him suffered for it. Dipendra "lifted him off the ground by the jaw. You didn't want to be on his bad side," someone remembered. [8]

Upon his return from Eton, Dipendra studied Geography and did his Masters from Tribhuwan University in Kathmandu. His Ph.D. thesis was on "Demographic Factors Affecting Fertility Among Migrants and Non-migrants in Kathmandu". Dr. Bal Kumar KC, his thesis supervisor, said he had known Dipendra since 1986 and never known him to be angry. When Kumar's wife died, Dipendra had sent a condolence message and a truck loaded with bamboo for the funeral. KC had travelled with Dipendra during his data collection trips and also given him lessons at the Tribhuwan Sadan, where the massacre took place many years later. KC never thought Dipendra was chain-smoker or that he had anything abnormal about him.[9]

Dipendra came of age in 1988 amid large-scale celebrations. Whenever King Birendra was away from the country, he acted as the Chairman of the Council of Royal Representatives. A poem he had written was published in a coffee-table volume on the occasion of the Queen's 50th birthday. Titled *Soldier*, it reads as follows:

Left bonds of affection, having duly understood,
If needed, soaked in blood, be ready to fight I will,
To flames reduce, will lightning halt, spray with blood I will,
On this uniform the country's sindur,
Shake this Earth I will.

The words seem to have been a self-fulfilling prophecy, although they brought him no glory. They came tragically true for the poet-prince on the night of June 1, 2001.

MONARCHY IN NEPAL

King Gyanendra has the unique distinction of having been crowned twice in a period of fifty years. The first time he was a three year-old child and remained King for two months. Back then, in 1951, the crowning was part of a larger political scene that he was too young to comprehend. He was fourth in the line of succession and yet the Kingship came to him. His grandfather, King Tribhuwan; his father, Mahendra; and his elder brother Birendra — all had greater claims on the throne than he did. All three were in New Delhi at the time, trying to break the dominance of the Ranas, the hereditary Prime

▼
King Gyanendra

88

Ministers of Nepal. The little Prince was left behind with his maternal grandfather, Hari Shamsher Rana. The then Rana Prime Minister, Mohan Shamsher Rana, called a meeting to declare that a new King must be chosen as the earlier King had suddenly left the country and the throne should not be left unoccupied. Hem Raj Sharma, the Deputy Royal Preceptor or the *Naib Badaguruju,* crowned the little boy. His son was to crown the same boy King for the second time fifty years later. However, no foreign country was willing to accept young Gyanendra as the new King of Nepal when his elder male relatives were still living. Finally, a compromise was worked out and the rightful King, Tribhuwan, was welcomed back to Nepal and occupied the throne once again.

▲
King Mahendra (1965)

The line of monarchy in Nepal is long and complex. There have been the usual palace intrigues that are common in any kingdom. The *Kot* Massacre of 1846 lives on in the memory of the people of Nepal, handed down from generation to generation. The then Prime Minister, Fateh Jung and several other court nobles were ruthlessly killed. King Rajendra

Queen Kanti Rajya Laxmi, Queen of King Tribhuwan and mother of King Mahendra.

Crown Princess Indra Rajya Laxmi (mother of King Birendra).

Bikram Shah had two queens at the time, named Samrajyalaxmi and Rajyalaxmi. The senior Queen's son, Surendra, was the Crown Prince. But the junior Queen, Rajyalaxmi, wanted that her son, Ranendra, be appointed heir apparent. Queen Rajyalaxmi had been given certain powers by the King. So she appointed Jung Bahadur, the Prime Minister, hoping to ensure that he would arrange for eliminating the Crown Prince to make way for her own son. Jung Bahadur was the first Rana Prime Minister of Nepal. But since he did not bother to fulfil her wishes after becoming Prime Minister, she plotted to have Jung Bahadur killed. Nepalese history remembers this story as *Bhandharkhal*. The Prime Minister learnt of the plot, however, and exiled the Queen to Varanasi, in India. The King accompanied her. He tried to raise a group that would overthrow Jung Bahadur but the troops were defeated near the Indo-Nepal border. This episode is known as *Alau Parba*. King Rajendra was brought to Nepal and confined in the Royal Palace of Bhaktpur. His son, Surendra, was crowned King. Jung Bahadur received the title of *Maharaja* and also the earlier principalities of Kaski and Lamjung. Thereafter the Kings were called *Shree Panch* (five times) *Maharajadhiraj*, and the Prime Ministers were called *Shree Teen* (three times) *Maharaj*.

There has been a tradition in the Royal family of marriage with the Rana family. In 1856, Prime Minister Jung Bahadur Rana had his two daughters, Tara and Lalit Rajya Laxmi, married to the Crown Prince Trailokya, who died without ever ascending the throne. Princess Lalit Rajya Laxmi had a son, Prithvi Bir Bikram, who was to occupy the throne in the future. King Prithvi Bir was the first King of Nepal to have Rana blood in him. He was married to two Rajput girls from the Indian state of Punjab. He also had two more wives. These two girls were sisters, the daughters of Prime Minister Bir Shamsher and his wife's maid Khanjan. Now, Lalit Rajya Laxmi, a Rana herself, did not want these Rana girls to bear a son who would go on to be Crown Prince. She devised an elaborate way to ensure that she had her way. The King used to visit his wives by turns each night. The nights he was to visit the Rana Queens, Lalit Rajya Laxmi made sure he encountered beautiful servant-girls before that. By the time he reached his real wives, he would be too exhausted to make his Queens pregnant. Perhaps Queen Aishwarya's attempts to manipulate Dipendra's marriage for her own purposes, as Lalit Rajya Laxmi had done in the past, precipitated the tragedy that befell the Shah dynasty.

▲
Queen Komal

▼
Queen Ishwari Rajya Laxmi Shah, Junior Queen of King Tribhuwan and mother of Prince Basundhara

▲
Crown Prince Birendra playing a "madal" in a party, 1971.

▶
King Birendra visiting Ilam in eastern Nepal is accompanied by the Queen. He was crown prince at that time and became King two months later. On the left is Colonel Bharat Kesar Singh who is the father of Anant Kesar Singh, the ADC of Queen Aishwarya at the time of the massacre.

Thus, the throne and the right to ascend it have always been matters of controversy in the past. That is true not only in Nepal but in all instances all over the world where the Crown and its accompanying power are involved. Gyanendra has ascended the throne for the second time, despite great odds. It is to be hoped that Nepal sees some political stability at last.

A DELICATE SITUATION

Nepal's situation at the moment is not enviable. The monarchy is under scrutiny, and threatened by powerful groups like the Maoist activists. The people are struggling to realign their trust in the new order. To add to it, there are problems Nepal has always suffered from. These include lawlessness, drug-abuse, smuggling and corruption. The new King has his hands full.

King Gyanendra was born on July 7, 1947, in the Narayanhiti Royal Palace of Kathmandu. Never having expected to be King, as Dipendra and Nirajan had a stronger claim on the throne, he had involved himself in other activities. He was educated at St. Joseph's College in Darjeeling, India. He graduated from Tribhuwan University, Kathmandu. He married Komal Rajya Laxmi Rana, the great grand daughter of Prime Minister Juddha Shamsher Rana. He has worked in the field of conservation and development,

▼
People paid tributes to the massacred King and Queen in different localities in Kathmandu by presenting bouquets of flowers.

as well as been a successful businessman. Chairman of the King Mahendra Trust for Nature Conservation, a non-profit NGO, he was actively involved in conservation projects in various parts of Nepal. Wildlife conservation has also been a concern of the organisation. On the business front, King Gyanendra, along with other members of the Royal family, owns most of the shares of the Soaltee group, which can boast of some of the best hotels in Kathmandu. After his crowning, Gyanendra declared his wife Komal to be the

Badamaharani, or Queen of Nepal. However, he did not proclaim his son, Paras, as the new Crown Prince. This is believed to be a careful decision, as Paras had been involved in a hit-and-run case last year that left a Nepalese musician dead. People had campaigned for action to be taken against Paras. The bereaved Nepalese population may not accept him as the Crown Prince at this time.

Long queues of mourners to sign condolence book outside the southeastern gate of Narayanhiti Palace.

There is a bigger problem confronting the Kingdom of Nepal at the moment. And that is the Maoist insurgency problem. The past ten years of flux on Nepal's political front has eroded the people's faith in that very

95

Nepalese riot police remove burning tires from a street in Kathmandu. Nepali authorities slapped another curfew on the capital to try to

parliamentary democracy which they had fought for eleven years ago. Thus a lot of popular support is directed towards the Maoists. Once King Birendra was declared dead, the Communist Party of Nepal (Maoist) announced that Nepal was now a Republic.

prevent further violence by protesters demanding the truth behind the massacre.

This, of course, is not a move that will magically solve the kingdom's problems at this point of time. The Maoists conducted a number of raids in the days immediately after the royal massacre. They attacked several police checkposts, killing policemen and grabbing lots of arms and ammunition. Accusations flew wildly. There were reports that the Deputy Chief of Mission of the Pakistan Embassy in Nepal had met with the Maoist leaders in Pokhara a few days earlier. The June 2, 2001 issue of a Pakistani newspaper called *Jung* alleged that the

▼ Nepalese riot police watch as people shout slogans against the new Nepalese king Gyanendra in front of the Royal Palace in Kathmandu.

Indian intelligence, RAW, had a hand in the massacre. It suggested that India had punished King Birendra for developing friendly relations with Pakistan and China. The leader of the Indian *Shiv Sena,* Bal Thackeray, said that Pakistan was the mastermind behind the killings.

The Maoists are quite influential in many districts of the hilly region in western Nepal. Over the past five years, a "People's War" had started which had gone on to claim almost two thousand lives. The insurgents had declared "liberated" or "base areas" in the regions that they controlled. They set up *Jana Adalat*, or People's Courts, in many areas to dispense justice. The judicial machinery of the state had not been functioning effectively in these places. They had even established their own revenue collection mechanisms, including a tax imposed on the salaries of government officials and schoolteachers. The leader of the Maoist movement in Nepal, Pushpa Kamal Dahal, had given himself the name of Comrade Prachanda.

After the King had been killed, Baburam Bhattarai, a Maoist leader, wrote an article in the leading publication, *Kantipur*.[10] In the article he praised King Birendra, and went on to say that his "crime" had been his patriotism and the liberal political views he held. Bhattarai wrote, "This was the biggest crime in the eyes of imperialists and expansionists." He said the King had preferred to bow before the wishes of his people in 1990 and hesitated to mobilise the army against the Maoist activists. Bhattarai blamed RAW and CIA for the killings and said these were India's political conspiracies to manipulate Nepal and get it to merge with India. He suggested that India would not encourage Maoist domination in Nepal and so had got rid of the King because he shared certain common approaches with the Maoists in Nepal. He exhorted the Royal Nepalese Army "not to support the puppet of expansionism born inside the palace." The editor of the daily, Yubaraj Ghimire, was arrested on charges of sedition for allowing such an inflammatory article in his newspaper.

Nepal's Prime Minister, Girija Prasad Koirala, was always rather unpopular. Just a few days before the killings, there was trouble in Nepal on his account. The people believed that he had made money off a deal on importing aircraft from Austria for Nepal's national airlines. Six communist parties had called for a *Nepal bandh*, a strike against the Prime Minister. Life had come to a standstill and had only just begun to recover the day of the killings, June 1. Even during the cremations and the days following the massacre, people rioted on the streets and shouted slogans against Koirala. Finally, on July 19, 2001, he resigned. The Indian newspaper, *The Pioneer*, flashed the headline, "Koirala can't contain Red upsurge; quits."[11] This had been Koirala's fourth term as Prime Minister. He is seventy-eight years old and finally resigned, as he admitted on state radio and television, "to make way for new initiatives to solve various problems facing the country."

After being crowned, one of the first things Gyanendra had done was to appoint an investigative team that would submit a report on the deaths of so many members of the Royal family. Several ADCs were dismissed from their posts. They included Sundar Pratap Rana, ADC to the King, Ananta Keshar Simha, ADC to the Queen, and Major Gajendra Bohra and Major Raju Karki, both ADCs to Dipendra. Several others were reprimanded for their inaction on the night of June 1. The Royal Task Force created after the

A Nepalese woman mourns in front of the Royal Palace in Kathmandu.

massacre has suggested that unauthorised arms should no longer be kept in the Palace complex. King Gyanendra has also banned the use of narcotics within the Palace. Security personnel can search members of the Royal family for the possession of weapons.[12]

It is true that the ADCs did not react speedily to the situation. There have been reports that perhaps they too had been having some narcotic substance that impeded their judgement and speed. Their testimony is inconclusive. All of them tried to enter the room where the firing was taking place but as the door was locked, they were considerably delayed. However, even after entering the room, their priority was to rescue the injured and take them to the hospital. None of them seem to mention trying to catch the man who was responsible for the shooting. It is also clear that no one admitted to having seen Dipendra shoot himself.

But the fact remains that no action could have been taken against Dipendra. He was, after all, the Crown Prince. As Dr. Ranjit Bhakta Pradhananga, a Nepali criminologist, has pointed out, "There is no provision in the Nepalese constitution." Thus Dipendra could not have had legal action initiated against him had he lived to face the consequences of his actions. Dr. Ranjit goes on to say, "He would have lost position only if he were invalid physically and mentally or if he were to renounce the Hindu faith."[13]

EPILOGUE

"What next?" That seems to be the question uppermost in all minds. The kingdom of Nepal needs some serious damage control measures immediately. The besieged nation must get back on track as soon as possible. The people desperately need to have their faith restored in some sort of effective administration. So far, the government of Nepal has not rallied positively to the people's aid. The Prime Minister himself resigned in the face of all these challenges, claiming to be making way for "new initiatives". It is unclear, however, where these initiatives that can save the future will come from. The Maoist insurgents seem to be in the reckoning for such leadership whether they are welcome or not. A lot of people, especially in certain western regions of Nepal, seem to be supportive of a Maoist takeover. That does not hold out the promise of solving too many problems either. Instead, lots of new, unforeseen problems may crop up in the wake of such a takeover. Whether to call in the national army against these Maoist forces or not seems to be the most crucial question at the moment.

The new monarch and the new Prime Minister need to win the people's trust. This, while not impossible, will certainly not take place overnight. If the people accept that Dipendra was the guilty party for the killings of June 1, they can begin to bury the past and move on to the future. However, as long as the doubts remain, it will be difficult to trust anyone. There are too many dark conspiracy theories doing the rounds. The report submitted by the Commission appointed for investigative purposes is seen to be too full of holes and contradictions. Devayani does not seem to be telling the whole truth. The testimony of the eyewitnesses is not conclusive. Every line of thought comes back to the starting point. It is quite obvious that people would like to blame someone other than a member of the Royal family for the cold-blooded killings. But the facts seem to point in the general direction of Dipendra as being the killer.

Nepal must hold out, in the near future, against threats from various factions. It must function successfully as the multi-party democracy that it claims to be and quell all dissenting voices effectively. The insurgency of the Maoists needs to be stamped out. That is a difficult undertaking, for they have popular support in so many areas. In order to eliminate this threat, the government has to first provide a viable alternative to the administrative network that the Maoists have established in the past five years. It is a gigantic project that will face several obstacles. But at this stage, Nepal has nothing left to lose. The King and the kingdom hold each other's fate in their hands.

APPENDIX

THOSE KILLED IN THE MASSACRE

1. King Birendra

Born in December 1945, he studied at St. Joseph's School in Darjeeling, India; Eton, Britain and Harvard, USA. At Harvard his teachers included Henry Kissinger and Samuel Huntington. He married Aishwarya in 1970. He ascended the throne of Nepal in January 1972 and the coronation took place in 1975. He ruled Nepal according to the Panchayat system for eighteen years until it changed to a constitutional monarchy in 1990.

2. Queen Aishwarya

She was born in November 1949 in Kathmandu. After her marriage, she gave birth to three children, Dipendra, Sruti and Nirajan. She was declared Queen or *Badamaharani* in 1972 when Birendra was crowned the King of Nepal.

3. Dipendra

Born in June 1971, he was educated at Budhanilkantha School and Eton. At the time of his death he was working on his Ph.D. He is believed to have killed nine members of his immediate family on June 1, 2001. He allegedly tried to commit suicide after killing them and eventually died two days later at the hospital. His body was taken to the cremation grounds under curfew conditions.

4. Sruti

Born to Birendra and Aishwarya in 1976, she was their only daughter. She had studied in Mayo College, Ajmer, India. She married Gorakh Shamsher Rana, grandson of Keshar Shamsher Rana. She is survived by her husband and two little girls.

5. Nirajan

He was the youngest son of Birendra and Aishwarya. He was born after the coronation of his father and had studied at Budhanilkantha School.

6. Princess Shanti Singh

She was born to King Mahendra and Indra Rajya Laxmi Shah in 1941. Her husband, Dipak Bahadur Singh, was the *Raja* of the Bajhang principality of western Nepal. She received her education at Darjeeling's Loreto Convent in India. She was involved in many social work projects and founded the Nepal Leprosy Association.

7. Princess Sharada Shah

She was Birendra and Shanti's sister, born in 1943. She studied at Loreto Convent in Darjeeling like her sister. Her husband was Kumar Khadga Bikram Shah.

8. Kumar Khadga Bikram Shah

Born in 1942, he was a scholar and the Director of the Centre of Nepal and Asian Studies at Tribhuwan University.

9. Dhirendra Shah

Born in 1950, he was King Mahendra's third son. His mother died when he was just one year old. He was married to Princess Prekshya Rana, Aishwarya's sister. They had three children. However, he divorced her to marry an English woman. As a result he had to give up his rights and property as a member of the Royal family.

10. Jayanti Shah

Born in 1948, she was the daughter of Prince Basundhara and Princess Helen.

THE LUCKY SURVIVORS

1. Princess Komal

She is the second daughter of Kendra Shamsher Rana and the younger sister of Queen Aishwarya. The wife of Gyanendra, she was declared the new Queen on June 4, 2001. She was slightly injured but was able to testify about the events of June 1 in front of the high-level inquiry commission.

2. Princess Shobha Shahi

The youngest daughter of King Mahendra, she is married to Mohan Bahadur Shahi.

3. Ketaki Chester

She is Prince Basundhara and Princess Helen's daughter. She left the Royal family because she divorced her first husband in order to marry a foreigner.

4. Kumar Gorakh Shamsher Rana

The husband of Princess Sruti, he was badly wounded but survived the attack. He is the second cousin of Devayani's father, Pashupati Rana.

5. Queen Mother Ratna Rajya Laxmi Shah

She was King Mahendra's second wife. She was declared Queen or *Badamaharani* when Mahendra ascended the throne in 1955. His first wife, Crown Princess Indra Rajya Laxmi Shah. was her sister. She was the granddaughter of the earlier

Rana Prime Minister, Juddha Shamsher Rana. She did not testify before the investigative committee.

5. Princess Helen Shah

She was married to Prince Basundhara and is the great granddaughter of Juddha Shamsher Rana (PM of Nepal, 1932-1945). During the shooting she was in the adjoining room with the Queen Mother and therefore remained unhurt.

6. Prince Paras

He is the only son of King Gyanendra. He testified before the committee as a witness. He is one of the few who was at the scene but was not even shot at. There was an instance two years back when he was involved in a hit-and-run accident and a person was killed. A huge petition had been submitted to the King to request that some action be taken against him.

7. Princess Himani

She is Prince Paras' wife and also escaped unhurt from the shooting.

8. Princess Prerana

She is King Gyanendra's daughter and sister to Paras.

9. Princess Puja

She is the daughter of Dhirendra Shah and Princess Preksha. She is married to Capt. Rajiv Shahi, the doctor who escaped safely and testified before the committee.

10. Princess Sitasma

She is the daughter of Dhirendra Shah and Princess Preksha. She was uninjured in the shootout.

11. Princess Dilasma

Another daughter of Dhirendra and Preksha, she too escaped unhurt that evening.

12. Ravi Shamsher Rana

The son of Juddha Shamsher Rana, he is married to one of King Tribhuwan's daughters. He was one of the last persons to speak to King Birendra that evening. The High Level Investigation Committee also listened to his testimony about the events.

13. Maheshwar Kumar Singh

Married to a daughter of King Tribhuwan, he was one of the first to arrive at the party. He was slightly injured in the massacre.

14. Rajiv Shahi

A doctor in the Nepal Army, he is married to Princess Puja. When the shooting intensified, he escaped through the window. He took a taxi to the Army Hospital and called a Press Conference two days later. There were reports that disciplinary action may be taken against him because he called for such a conference without getting any approval beforehand.

NOTES

[1] *Budhbar*, June 27, 2001.

[2] *Jana Astha*, June 13, 2001.

[3] *Ghatana ra Bichar*, June 27, 2001.

[4] *Bimarsha*, June 8, 2001.

[5] *The Hindustan Times*, India, June 11, 2001.

[6] *Ghatana ra Bichar*, June 27, 2001.

[7] *Rajdhani*, June 11, 2001.

[8] *Sunday Times*, London, June 3, 2001.

[9] *Saanghu*, June 18, 2001.

[10] June 6, 2001.

[11] July 20, 2001.

[12] *Rajdhani*, July 7, 2001.

[13] *Deshantar*, June 24, 2001.